# Introduction

Today's market place is very different than forty-years ago. Forty-years ago if you wanted to open a business you had to have upfront costs, property, large amounts of inventory, and your best bet for advertising was the local paper and direct mail pieces. Of course, this took a lot of effort and even more money. You had to hope and wait for people to get your ad and decide to come and purchase a product from you. Going out and getting them to come into your store would have been a difficult feat.

Additionally, forty-years ago your ability of growth was limited to local purchasers for the most part. If what you had to offer was not in a reasonable distant from your potential consumers, your company suffered. Moreover, because most shopping was done near home, any bad publicity could really hurt your company's reputation; thus, leading to your company being shut down.

Forty-years ago consumers had to find local places to purchase their goods at; everyday shopping was done within a modest radius from home-base. To know what merchant had new products or sales, one had to wait for either the Wednesday Flyer or the Sunday paper. Options for product purchases barely existed beyond one's living area.

Jump forward to the modern day and we know all of this has changed. Today, any individual can purchase whatever they desire from anywhere in the world. Most likely shipping will be free and the products returnable. There is nothing that cannot be found – the Internet has everything from the rarest of coffees to cheap rubber bracelets. It does not matter what is wanted, it is there for the purchase. And, that ability to purchase whatever it is wanted can be comparison shopped in the blink of an eye; thus an environment that is exceptional for the buyer and a tough one for merchants.

For business owners the Internet can be hit or miss. There are more customers than one can shake a stick at with an equal amount of competition. Unlike yester years when your nearest competition was a decent amount of distance away and your location added to your bottom for consumers appreciate convenience; the Internet has competition that is breathing down your neck. Competition on the Internet is so close to your proximity that it would seem your could just reach right through the Internet and touch them. They can take tease your customer away long before that customer ever knows you exist. In fact, all your competition has to do is rank better then you on any search engine results page.

Understanding the importance of your competitions proximity is one of the most important things to understand when dealing with marketing attempts on the Internet. Today, there is no distance between you and your competition and you most likely have anything that can not be bought on some other website. Now, when a consumer wants and needs a product or information, all they must do is put there desires into the URL and pages among pages of options displays on the search engine results page.

What you must be concerned with in this situation, when listed amongst your competitors is stand out. In this book, you will learn about the main and most popular techniques to purchasing traffic to you website.

We will discuss pay-per-click methods that are one of the very most popular formats to use. This technique works nicely and if you create an excellent ad, you will gain enough traffic to push you to the next level of success. We will also discuss banner ads that were the first on the block for website marketing ads. They fell from popular use for awhile but in the last few years they have made their way back due to technological advances. These are inexpensive and if done write, valuable.

To add to your arsenal of marketing weapons, we will also discuss email marketing and Search Engine Optimization. Email marketing is a great tool and excellent for targeted marketing attempts when you want to get up-close and personal with potential customers. Email marketing, if done well, will build your own client lists that will prove profitable.

Search Engine Optimization is the king of purchasing website traffic. Search Engine Optimization is not purchasing traffic in the traditional means of the online market place. However, it is worth more than its weight in gold when done properly. Search Engine Optimization can bring in traffic like no other technique and those who understand its value can become the master of their search engine results page listing and rank. What is so pertinent to understanding this technique is that it can eventually lead to you not needing to pay for traffic from other mediums as all. Of course, you will continue to want to use other methods of paid website traffic, but you will be able to become much more selective in your efforts with more to spend on growth.

We will end this book with terms you need to know to start understanding the web marketing industry. When first learning how to build your web site, it can be hard to gather your thoughts and wrap your mind around what is being said. To help in that, terms that are most often discussed in web traffic buying is listed. Not all of these terms are concepts mentioned throughout the book, but they are listed to add to your understanding. Read them as you would the rest of the book. They provide more than just definitions, there are helpful tips to be garnered.

# Chapter 1
# PAY-PER-CLICK (PPC)
# ADVERTISING CAMPAIGNS

## What It Is

Advertising through the PPC method allows you as a business owner to place ads with keyword usage within search engine result pages, of course, for a price. The goal of PPC is to help website business owners attract targeted customers. Target customers are those that are already looking for your product offerings or the similar; this helps you by putting your ads and business in front of those who are most likely potential buyers. The goal of PPC methods of advertising is to provide you, the site owner, to control your budget while still gaining maximum site exposure.

Understand, you do not pay for the placement of your ad; instead, you pay once a potential customer clicks on your ad and goes onto your website. The amount you pay for that customer has already been agreed to through a bidding system. It is imperative to your site's success to appreciate that you are paying each and every time your link is hit and your landing page is accessed – remember your budget!

When first starting out with your PPC campaign you must keep an eye on your budget and be prepared to spend a bit more during your first few weeks while you learn the system. Once you have your funds ready, it is time to determine your keywords. Make sure you properly research not only the best keywords or keyword phrases, but also the value of those words in terms of competition. Move onto creating your ad and creating an account and before you know it, you will have plenty of data to help you steer your efforts.

Often times, third-party companies allow for ads from search engines to be placed on their site; these are often referred to as a content network property. This is a benefit for all involved; especially considering it is not often in life you get a situation is win-win-win. See, the third-party gets a portion of the revenue paid by you the advertiser. In fact, they can earn upwards of eighty percent. Consider when you have searched for an item or information on the web and landed on a website full of information; remember the ads that are on the page? These ads usually have something in common and complementary with the item or information you sought.

It is not uncommon for consumers to ignore the ads on the content network and this place is not nearly as valued as listing high on the search engine results page. When your ads appear on a content network property, do not be concerned – your ad is still being seen! In fact, your ad is being displayed and seen along side similar or complementary information to your product. Now, there may not be a high click through rate, but these searchers will most likely resemble your target audience and therefore, resemble your customers.

## Types of PPC

There are mainly two different types of PPC, flat rate and bid-based.

## Flat-rate

Flat rate is an excellent option, especially if you are selling products at great prices. This is often the option selected by those who have a need to show-up in the comparison shopping results page. On these types of search engines, customers are highly targeted along with the choice of product with minimal rates.

Remember, you can always pay more for higher ranking, but you may find you do not need to after gathering some baseline data for comparison. Question if paying more will actually gain you any more attention than the current or if changing your ad would prove wiser.

If you decide that you want to change your ad or even pay more for a higher level of exposure, check to see if that site uses rate cards. Rate cards have a fixed amount due per click but are according to the possible areas available as advertising space. Now, do not assume you are restricted to those prices only; no, you can negotiate if you are offering the search engine owners a long-term and valuable contract.

## Bid-based

Bid-based provides you the buyer lots of opportunity to control your budget; this type of PPC is like an auction for advertisers. Each PPC client informs the networks how much they are willing to pay to rank higher on the search engine results page – you set the maximum amount you are willing to pay and compete against other advertisers. The competition is conducted as an auction and each advertiser bids for the spot and you dropout when the bid has become too high for your budget. Often there are several spots open and this is often dependent on keyword. When there are several spots, they will be put in value order of the bid and perhaps ad quality – make great ads!

## Budgets & Bids

You will have to determine what your max rate will be when using PPC; when making this determination remember to consider that the web is open 24 hours a day 365 days a year. If you do not take the prior into consideration, you will find that PPC can get very expensive really quick. While you try to make this economically tough decision, try Yahoo's Estimator Tool. This tool will help you develop and calculate possible budgets and is very useful in judging how much money you will spend to take on your competitors and if it will be worth it. Overall, you want to spend enough to grow into the top five spots in the search engine results page.

You will also have to consider the value of your bid in terms of keywords. Some keywords are worth more than others are; in fact, some of the most popular keywords will prove almost impossible to afford. The affordability of a keyword has much to do with the financial power of your competitors, especially national brands. In these situations, you may want to look for keywords that are very specific so that when your ad does get clicked on your chances of conversion is greater.

## Preparing Your Ad

When preparing your ad, make sure you consider your audience. Take the time to learn their language, their hobbies, their hangouts, and their demographics; doing this will provide with a great deal of knowledge. This knowledge will gear your ad in the right direction to create eye-catching ads that get attention that leads to conversions.

Do not forget to make your ad and landing page cohesive so searchers know they have landed at the right place. Additionally, make sure the ad links to the information that the potential customer is seeking or your bounce rate will be higher than you desire.

## The Big Three

There are many different search engines on the Web that offer PPC, but the big three include Google AdWords, Yahoo! Search Marketing, and Microsoft adCenter.

## Google AdWords

Google AdWords is the largest player in the world of PPC. Because Google has built itself to be the most popular search engines and aims for customer satisfaction, it has the most possible amount of potential customers. The

amount of clients possible is astounding –
make a great ad and landing page and success
can be yours. Start here with your endeavors;
it is the easiest to manage and has plenty of
instructions available to help you gain your
PPC roots. It is worth noting that becoming
successful on any search engine site takes time
and effort; take the time to learn each PPC's
system.

**Yahoo! Search Marketing**

With more and more people turning to the
Internet to do their shopping it is a good idea
for people and businesses that are looking to
sell products and expand their consumer base
to have a presence online. This can be done
with the help of Yahoo! Search Marketing.
This program allows people or businesses to
advertise on the search results page on Yahoo!
And popular websites throughout the Yahoo!
Network.

If you decide to set up a Yahoo! Search
Marketing account, you can use what they call
a "sponsored search" to make advertisements
that contain keywords that you think that
people will use when they search for a
business like yours. When the keywords that
you have chosen match what is put into the
search engine, your advertisement will appear
on the Yahoo! search results page. Then if all

the person doing the search has to do is click on the ad and they will be sent to your website.

A nice feature about Yahoo! Search Marketing is that you are in control of how much money you want to spend on your advertising. All you have to do is set a maximum bid of how much you are willing to pay when your ad is clicked, at the same time you can set the limit of what you want to spend each day. So you will not be hit with an astronomical bill out of the blue. This is a good option if you want to start out with just a little bit of advertising to see how it goes before deciding if you what to spend on advertising in the future or find that there may be somewhere else where you would be better off spending your budget.

## Microsoft adCenter

Microsoft adCenter is similar to Yahoo! Search Marketing accept it works with Microsoft's search engine, Bing. With Microsoft adCenter you can target your desired demographic of customers by using over ten thousand keywords, which you can apply to reach customers locally, by gender, and age range. By being able to hone in on your target demographic you will have the best opportunity to maximize your return on the investment that you have made with advertising.

When you use Microsoft adCenter, they will provide you with data that will help you and your company streamline your advertising campaign to ensure that you know when you are getting the maximum benefit and reaching the most customers. Microsoft ad Center is a pay-per-click advertising model. To get started using the program you set a maximum bid of what you are willing to pay for each click on your ad. You will also set up a monthly budget of what you are willing to spend on your advertising. Make sure that you keep that in mind when you are determining how much you want to spend for the month, if it turns out its too little your budget may be gone in less than a week, especially if the advertising campaign is more successful than you may think. So, make sure you take the time to think through it and do not be afraid to ask Microsoft for help in determining how much you should allocate to advertising.

## Chapter 2

## Banner Marketing

### What It Is

Banner marketing is designing and placing

ads on different websites that are selling products complementary to your own, which the ads are then embedded into your desired site. These ads were one of the first types of advertising used on the web; these ads were traditionally 468x60 pixels. This size made the ad easy to place on the majority of websites at the time. However, today's banner ads have many more sizes than in the past; much of this is due to technology allowing more sophisticated ads to be developed.

Banner ads are not a favorite of anyone in general and thus they have lost much of their gusto at the opening of the 21st century; in which PPC ads took over. Advertisers did not like banner ads because they are viewed as annoying by consumers and because the have a very low click-through-rate. Consumers do not like them because they can be annoying and poorly designed. Web hosts do not like them because they earn them very little economical reward for hosting. At one time, these ads were king, but today, they are seen as leftovers from a bygone era.

It should be noted that everyone's "favorite" pop-up ads are considered banner ads. As you know, everyone hates pop-ups and it would seem that at least half the planet spent millions on pop-up blockers. Surely, you have noticed that today they are rarely if ever seen.

When you are just starting out with a new website or new to the paid traffic marketing model, banner ads are not a bad way to go. The rates for these have continuously gone down over the years and thus, a great opportunity for a website owner with a limited budget and wanting to attempt several avenues of potential revenue.

Now banner ads may not make you rich but the truth is much of the success associate with banner ads have to do with design. In the past, these ads have been clunky, unattractive, and overwhelming to the eye of the viewer. Nevertheless, today, after tons of research has been done; one can design ads that are much more complementary to the host's site, easier on the eyes of the viewer, and a better representation of your company and offerings.

Of course, design is not the only aspect to be concerned about, it is equally important to be concerned with ad placement. You do not want to have your ads in front of an audience that is not looking for products not related to yours. This would be a wasted audience that is not targeted at all, let alone a waste of funds. Trust combining great design, great placement, and low costs can lead your company into an excellent return rate on investment.

Your goal should always be to spend less and less on advertising efforts over time. Note, once you have gained a good footing on the search engine result page, along with several free ways to advertise, your advertisement spending will become less and less while or organic search engine result page placement increases.

Once you have placed your banners in different websites, it is important that you also keep track of their performance. Check which of the banners are performing well and learn from the ones that are not doing so well.

**Banner Ad Design**

As stated earlier, banner ads need to be designed in a manner that is appealing and non-intrusive. That said; they need to be creative but not gaudy and attention grabbing but not overly flashy to make potential customers curious enough to click it. This is not the only aspect in design to be concerned about; it is equally important to give attention to fonts and message. If the font is difficult to read or overwhelming people will not want to bother with reading your ads. Keep your message short and simple so the effort spent by potential purchasers is understood quickly and thoroughly.

Remember, to gain a high click through rate that leads to higher conversions through the use of banner ads remember the success of your ad relies on the following four factors: relevance, size, design, and positioning. Relevance as discussed above simply means that your ad appears on a page that has something in common what you are offering. Size, avoid making your ad as large as you can; keep the ad reasonable to the size of a computer screen. Do not make it two small either; you do want people to notice it, use common sense and attractiveness as a guide. Keep your design elements clean and simple; do not design the ads to be flashy. Position the ad to where it will be most attractive on the page according to its size. If your ad is on the larger size, aim for the ad to be displayed across the top of the page or down the right side. If it is a smaller ad, aim for the right-hand side on the upper half of the page.

## Banner Advertising Costs

Costs are usually calculated per click through with the contract lasting a month. The cost of banner ads are a bit different than PPC in that the costs are usually per thousand impressions and that costs can be as little as $25 per thousand. But remember, if you have developed your ad right, you may find you have received a thousand hits in just a day or two with your banner ads.

However, it is worth noting, that after a few weeks to a month you will see your click rate begin to diminish. This is because people get use to seeing your ad and already know what it is and no longer find value in it. Thus, it is important to have several ads that you can rotate to keep the purchasers attention fresh. Additionally, because your company name should be on all ads it will appear that there is something new to visit- branding works, use it.

Because there is the chance you do a great job creating an ad you must pay attention to the costs and the value of each costs. If you find that you have done a great job and receiving a high-level of click-through you may want to consider another option for your banner ads. Another option would be banner exchanging in which websites agree to share space on one another sites. This can be a great option and it can save more than a few bucks.

More importantly is that you can choose who you want to exchange with; thus, you can really get close to your targeted audience. Now you may be wondering why not just start with an exchange system instead of paying – it is a reasonable thought. However, just like you can select what site to be on so can others. You want to choose sites with good reputations, a nice level of customers, and those that intend to build their own site into a success. They will want to do the same so it is imperative that you build-up up some for of popularity so others will want you as "company". Additionally, the better and the more popular your site becomes, the more your ad is shown on the site you exchanged with. If you initiated the exchange, you will be able to have your ad shown for slightly above the rate you will provide for the exchange. For example, if you agree put your exchanger as 20 times, you can expect yours to be shown about 13 times and the more popular you site become the more the reciprocal number increases,

**Banner Ad Tips**

> ➢ Keep the message and the font style and size simple and easy to read.

> ➢ Do not forget to ad a call-to-action tactic – tell you customers what to do and hope they follow through. If you can add the word "free", your click through rate will be higher than without. Who doesn't love free things?

➢ Do not loose the opportunity to associate your banner ad colors with your product design colors- this will help with your branding efforts. When you consider that the click rate can be less than one percent, assume the most desirable effects of banner ads is getting your brand recognized.

➢ Never use banner ads as your sole avenue of advertising; instead, use it as an augmenting and complementary method within your advertising campaign.

➢ Use some type of animation, but do not over do it; simply ad enough to gain the eye's attention.

➢ If you are advertising on information page containing news and the like use a static type ad, which usually works better on such host sites.


## Chapter 3
## Email Marketing

**What It Is**

One can liken email marketing as direct market for the Internet; just like you get all that mail in your mailbox at home you get electric email in your email account. The goal is to communicate with your current or potential customers that can develop into a relationship between you as the seller and the email recipient as the buyer. This is important to understand considering that this relationship can build repeat and loyal customers that will seek your email information out and read what you are currently offering every time you send an email out.

What is go great about email marketing is that for a relatively low-cost investment, especially when compared to the costs of direct mail pieces you get in your home's mailbox. Additionally, you can reach a remarkable amount of email account owners; with the overwhelming majority checking their email at least once a day. Moreover, you can easily track your email campaigns to tweak them to perfection.

This very large industry does have a few issues though. There is a constant struggle in creating communications that are perceived as genuine and sincere that leads to an actionable reaction by the reader. Additionally, there is the issue of proper design elements that grab the reader's attention without being overdone and garish.

When it comes to building a constant relationship with your readers, you must also consider building and managing your database. The information garnered from your relationship is priceless; thus, you must be able to analyze data in such a way as you continue to calibrate your message and offerings in such a way as to economically build your company's financial baseline. To help you, there are many programs and companies available that offer database marketing software to not only help you build your database, but will help you analyze, automate, and execute your email marketing attempts. These programs are very important to your success especially when you consider that you gaining emails from many avenues in your traffic generation campaign. Being able to sort and control your data while being able to analyze responses, and automate both notifications and responses saves you time and money.

One area of concern with any email campaign is being viewed as SPAM. SPAM is not just a concern for small, unknown companies; large nationally known companies cannot buy themselves out of this one. If an email recipient does not recognize your company or has not opted-in to receiving your emails they will either delete your email or put it in the junk mail bin. Thus, it is always best to use email marketing as an augmentation to your overall traffic generation campaign to gain more opt-ins from potential customers. An additional benefit to opt-in email is that you can become very personal with your customers and both parties; you and them, are happy with the relationship. But remember, offer an opt-out button as well; this makes people feel better and safer about the relationship.

Now email marketing, especially when it is an opt-in, as mentioned above, is the ability to get personal with your customers. You can keep them up-to-date with everything going on with your business; thus, making your clients an emotional stakeholder. Send them thank you cards, newsletters, special events invites; your imagination is the limit on how integrated you can become with your customers.

With all the benefits of email marketing, you do have to be concerned with a few legal issues, covered below.

**Legal Issues**

In America, there is the CAN-SPAM Act of

2003. This Act was passed to stop email marketers from using false information, false subject lines, etc. Know that there can be a fine upward of $16K per email per account. Make sure you always check the development of this and other similar laws as they change frequently.

The Directive on Privacy and Electronic Communications was introduced the marketing behavior of business by the European Union in 2002. You must be concerned with Article 13 of this directive, which prohibits the use of email addresses for marketing uses. From this directive, the opt-in concept was developed. Because many nations have embraced some form of this directive it is important that you research and become aware of all nation's law's in which you plan to send emails.

**Designing Your Email**

Make sure you create a great tag line to get that email opened. Within the email, keep the design and writing simple and clean. Make sure you get to the point of things immediately, know one wants to spend several paragraphs worth of reading time to find they are not interested – they will tell their friends, and so on. For example, if you are having a sell, design so that percentage off is upfront and noticeable. Also, if you like, you can embed email videos or the like to ad enticement.

Adding video to your emails have become common place and easy to create due to technology. If you do not have all the equipment and expertise, do not worry, there are many sites available to help you with their systems. Additionally, many email readers like the video email types; they seem more personal to many, this is especially true with younger demographics that are accustom to such current technologies.

Basic email marketing and video emails are not your only options, try audio postcards. Audio postcards add that extra edge that can really get your website and products noticed. Again, there are many sites available to help you set such an email campaign that leads to profits.

Remember, develop several different ads to not only test for which will be the most received and action has been taken, but to ensure your image stays fresh and appealing. Do not forget to add the opt-out link.

## Get That Email Opened

You know that just about everyone has an

email account and currently on this topic, those are the only ones you should be concerned about. No matter your great offerings or intent, you still have to get your emails opened to create sells. There are four areas of concern when it comes to a great email campaign: the subject line, the product, the offer, and the copy.

The subject line needs to offer the reader a great tease to bring them to click further into the email. Keep the subject short and sweet; get straight to the point without giving to much information away. If you give too much information away there will be little reason for someone to read the email any further – they have already made their decision. Another touch is to use the recipient's first name. This may seem obvious to people but it is often overlooked. Remember, you want your ads to be personal. You could also ask the recipient a question or if there is a problem that you can solve for them with your product.

When it comes to products make sure what you are offering goes to email recipients that need that product – selling baby strollers to those without children is fruitless for you and of course, a waste of time and money. This is also the case with the offer. If you are selling a baby stroller at a steep discount to those earning over $250k per annually, you may find a low conversion rate. This is because these individuals earn enough to not be overly concerned with sales. However, if your strollers are the newest high-end types that are hard to find – send that campaign out to these parents immediately. Now for that same discount mentioned above, recipients earning less than $50k per year are much more likely to open the email and take action. Offer what is needed!

When it comes to the email copy, keep it easy, simple, memorable, and casual. Casual writing like using one's first name, keeps the email personal. Make sure your email is quick to read as well; use bullet lists to get your point across and provide the facts and just the facts, nothing else is needed. Also, ensure there is plenty of whitespace to the ad so it does not seem crowded and poorly designed.

When it comes to the call to action do not be pushy. Tell the recipient the truth, if you only have 10 products left and let them know when those 10 are gone the offer will be ended. On the other hand, perhaps, you want to inform your recipients that the sale is just on for a certain time frame. Regardless of what your offer limitations are, be open honest, and do so without being pushy, rude, or insincere.

**Costs of Mailing Lists**

You will need a mailing list to start out with the hopes of gaining a massive amount of opt-ins. To get one, call upon a mailing list broker. What is great about the use of a broker is that they can help you narrow down your list to your desired and targeted customer. This is important because you don't want to was your money sending emails or purchasing a list that provides a return on investment rate that serves your company nil.

So, how can a broker help you narrow down and reach out to your target market? Perhaps you seek men between the ages of twenty-five and fifty, who earn at least $80k per year that purchases weight-lifting equipment, within a fifty mile radius of your brick and mortar store. Brokers can make it happen. Note, that the more broken down the list the more expensive it can get. But don't let the worry you. Yes, it will be more expensive than a basic list; but, it will provide you with the most responsive and likely customers who lead to a better rate of return.

Mailing lists are usually sold by the thousands, so perhaps, five thousand names for anywhere from $50 - $400 per list. Now, if you plan on purchasing on a monthly base, you may be able to negotiate the costs or perhaps an increase of names. You will want to make a monthly purchase until you are stable; if you can not, don't worry, growth takes time.

## Chapter 4
## SEO & Web-Content

### SEO

All too often business owners fail to understand the importance of SEO and web-content, when in fact, it may just be the most important thing one can do when purchasing website traffic. This is different from the other techniques discussed in that the "payment" goes directly into your own business. Understanding SEO will lead you to understanding the value of excellent web-content.

### What It Is

SEO is Search Engine Optimization and it is king. In today's world of online marketing, anyone ignoring SEO is bound to fail. This marketing technique is the best and most efficient option available to getting massive amounts of traffic to your website. As stated above, the payment for this traffic is in the development of your own business instead of paying someone else for bringing traffic to you. Do not misunderstand; you do have to pay just differently than the prior strategies discussed. Let us delve into understanding SEO. The best way to understand why you would purchase such help as SEO, you must understand how it works, we will take this step-by-step.

First, you must understand that all information searched for on the web is categorized in some format or another and when an individual puts in term to be searched for the computer goes through its files to find pertinent information. This information is then displayed on the search engine results page. Of course, you must be wondering how the computer can gather and sort so much information in under a second. The answer is referred to as "spiders".

As with all creatures spiders must be fed and this not so living spider is no different except these spiders eat words. Web spiders are automated scripts that visit different URLs looking for the perfect matches within the site itself. When the proper information isn't found, the spider crawls through all the links within the site onto the next, again with the desire to seek the correct information.

What is the correct information? The correct information is the information that most accurately matches the search term. Now it is not that simple because we are talking about an exchange of information.

What is the correct information? The correct information is the information that most accurately matches the search term. For your information to be selected as the correct information, you must use keywords not only in your web-content but in the web-architecture as well. This is why you hear so much about key words; key words feed the spiders and if your content is properly written and kept constant than the spiders will love stopping in for a bit. This is important because by feeding the spiders, you gain page-rank organically by constantly being indexed by search engines and thus able to be pickier about other advertising methods. If you don't get indexed, the spiders assume you don't exist!

Now, if you are offering products versus information, it is doubly important for you to have some type of web-content. You must have something for the spiders to eat. If you are wondering what content you could use for, let us say a wok, all you have to do is create some guides. How about a wok cooking guide? Perhaps a guide informing readers on the different types of woks available is an excellent choice. Maybe, a wok cookbook or a wok cookbook for vegetarians could be offered to readers? As you see, there are option regardless your product. What is nice about offering guides is that you can have potential customers download it immediately and voluntarily opt-in to your marketing campaigns; this will build your email campaign list.

So, what does all this have to do purchasing big web-site traffic? Keep reading and you will learn the money spent h with this technique will serve you better than all the rest combined and perhaps, even cost less.

## Keywords

The use of keywords within SEO is the heart of SEO and SEO is the heart of online marketing. It is with keywords that spiders find you and rank you. Keywords represent what you offer on your site and what others would type in a search engine to find their needs. There are plenty of companies available to help you in this area, both fee-based and free. When you are first starting off, it is best to select a fee-based company until you are able to learn how to use the free tools. In fact, when using a fee-based company to get started, ask lots of questions and attempt to use the free tools to come up with the same results.

When picking your keywords take the time to

brainstorm all the possibilities and don't forget to include phrases. They should be relevant in that the rest of your content has something to do with the keywords and of value to the reader. Now, the keywords you use should have lots of searches but low amount of competition; this can be hard especially for an item that is popular.

Keywords are not just for web-content, you must use them per site page. Keyword placement is used within item descriptions, tags, copy, page titles, description tags, Meta keywords tag, headings, navigational links, and every single thing you place on your site. This can be difficult since you must know at least the basics of computer coding to get it right. If you have yet to start or at just the beginning of building your site, get someone involved immediately instead of waiting to later. This will save you tons of money in having a coder going in and trying to fix everything. Additionally, when just starting out your site will probably be small with just a few pages to about 20, this allows the cost of SEO site development less costly as well. By doing things this way, you can have new pages done as needed so you don't have tons of cash on hand – pay as you go.

A quick note about keywords that should be heeded; do not use what is called "keyword stuffing". Keyword stuffing is when a keyword is on the page far too often and the keyword density is high, usually more than 8 percent of the total volume of web-content. When this happens it is considered poor taste and spiders will not only ignore your page, if in a bad mood, they will push your page further down the search engine results page.

## Web-content

Web-content is anything on you website and as you know it should have been written with SEO in mind. Once you know your keywords and phrases figured out you will need to develop you web-content. As mentioned above, you do not want any more than 5 keywords per page, so your web-content for that page should revolve around those keywords. Remember, you want the spiders to stop and read your pages.

When creating your web-content make sure that you use everyday language that the average individual within your targeted market segment could easily understand. You also want the web-content to sound natural and not stuffed with keywords that come across as pushy. You will also want each page to have its own theme. This will help keep your readers on your site and coming back in the future.

You will also want to keep the content relevant to what is currently happening in society. If you have a technology website and a new technology is coming out have that information on your site. If you keep your information up-to-date you will find that the same viewers are returning to visit your site for information. If you sell technological devices offer everything you can to help those seeking a particular product and offer news briefs on the additions to that product. As you do this, you will become a trusted agent in selling devices and information. Return customers are always the best and should be treated as such – send a special coupon to your returning customers. Remember, they tell their friends.

Creating a great web-content can be difficult; this is especially true when it comes to ensuring such content is aimed at search engine optimization. Do yourself a favor and have articles, press releases, white papers, documents, sale sheets and so on written by individuals that understand writing with search engine optimization in mind. These individuals understand the "rules" of SEO and can help you gain organic search engine results that will overtime lessen you marketing budget needs.

You will want organic search engine results,

not only will it lessen your marketing budget needs, but it will provide, overtime, a more permanent standing with the spiders. Favor with the spiders as mentioned earlier has endless value. The two easiest ways to gain favor with the spiders as we know is relevant material and keywords. It will save you time, money, and prove more progressive towards your goals to use a writer.

There are many avenues to finding a writer, just type in SEO writers into your URL and many individuals and companies will be displayed. The cost can from low to high. Make sure you know what you want in your writer. Do you want a native English speaker? Maybe, you want a writer you is also an excellent researcher. Perhaps, an individual that can write just about anything or maybe, a writer that can write scholarly and highly-academic works. Whatever you need in your writing areas, take the time to look around at different individuals and companies.

When it comes to writers and SEO needs, choose a writer you can supply repeat business to. This will serve you well. First, a writer that builds a relationship with a client and can expect monthly or more work assignments will always put you first on their lists of "to-dos". You can not under appreciate or take this for granted for there will come a time when a major event has taken place and you will need that writer immediately. Perhaps some important technology news or product must be up on your site as soon as possible. Or, maybe, you forgot about ordering that press release you so desperately need. You will find a good relationship with your SEO will not only be beneficial to getting things done, but you will also enjoy the benefits of that writer getting to know your needs and business. You may find they have ideas that can help you grow or associates that can help you in other areas.

## SEO & Web-content Tips

➢ Keep content relevant, fresh and attractive spiders – remember relevant and fresh material brings the spiders to your links.

➢ Pay attention to the language used for your offerings; this includes understanding demographics by age and how they would view and thus, refer to your product as.

➢ Always check what your competitors and doing and attempt to figure out the keywords they are using and how often they are adding new content to their

- site.

- Keep keyword usage in content towards the upper half of you site pages and within the first 300 words of the content – spiders only go so far down the page.

- Spiders can not read Flash so do not bother with it as a SEO attempt although, you can still add them to your site, just don't count on them in terms of SEO.

- Good content is written well – use a professional that know about SEO.

- Stay away from highly graphic pages – even if there is SEO content on that page, spiders will simply ignore the page.

- When linking with other sites, use the links within the web-content so spiders can follow easily and quickly – this will help you rank higher as well.

- Only link with reputable sites, if you link with sites that are considered poor, the spiders will ignore you.

- ➤ Don't assume you know what potential customer will refer to your offerings as, research your keywords to create keyword rich web-content.

- ➤ Keep web-content language simple and easy to understand.

- ➤ Opt for keywords that are highly searched by with low competition.

- ➤ Keep keywords within the first 200-300 words of your web-content.

- ➤ Never have more than five keywords per web page.

- ➤ Make sure each web-content page has a theme.

- ➤ The title tag is at the top of your web page, it should be no more than 12 words long.

- ➤ Meta descriptions tags are also at the top of your web page and should be no longer then 24 words long.

- ➢ Meta keywords tags is a t the top of the webpage in the head section where you can place all your keywords for the page, keep this no more to 48 words.

- ➢ Keep content such as articles or press releases under 500 words.

## Terms to Know

**A Tag Cloud:** A tag cloud is a cluster of tag words, usually in a box, with the most popular or important tags in a larger font or in bold type.

**Auto Bidding:** In auto bidding a bid that you have placed on a certain keyword increases one cent if the competitor that is closest to your bid changes theirs. You can set a maximum that you are willing to pay so if the bidding is not competitive you could pay less than you expected.

**Backlink:** A link that comes to your website from another website is known as a backlink. Backlinks are important because if they good links and sufficient in number they will affect your websites ranking due to search engine optimization and the significance that some search engines apply to backlinks.

**Bid:** A bid when related to keywords is the amount that you want to pay to be associated with certain advertisements that are matched with a keyword. After the bidding process is complete the bids are reviewed with the highest bids chosen and the advertisement and its message are shown in the order of the bids from highest to the lower bids that were accepted.

**Bounce Rate:** The Bounce Rate is really important because it tells you the number of people that visited your site and then decided to leave without going any further into the site. The most important aspect to this for you as a site owner is "Is my landing page the problem"? If you see a high bounce rate; say, above 50% you will want to test a new landing page set-up. Remember, your goal is a high conversion rates.

**Click-Through Rate (CTR):** Click-Through Rate refers to the amount of people that visited a website and have clicked on an advertising banner. Click-Through Rates are measured in percentages to show how successful an online advertising campaign was or is. The more successful the advertising campaign the higher the Click-Through Rate will be. To determine a Click-Through Rate you will have to know the number of visitors to the website, the number of times the advertisement was clicked and the number of times that the advertisement was displayed.

**Click-throughs:** This happens when a potential customer decides to go to your site from your placed ad. It's important to pay attention to this because it will inform you of how your placement on the search results page is affecting your business. Additionally, this will provide some idea of what you can do to appear higher on the page so you are noticed more often by those searching your keyword.

**Content Management Systems (CMS):** Content management systems is software that helps company's to easily create, edit, and publish electronic text. Content management systems that have been designed to publish on the Internet will help to pick out keywords and meta tags to help with search engines.

**Conversion Funnel:** This is the process that potential customers must go through to access your goods – keep it simple!

**Conversion Rate:** Conversion rate refers to the amount conversions that your website receives matched with the number of visitors you get to your site. This is used as a way of seeing if your website is successful. Important conversion rates to consider on your website are the number of sign ups for newsletters, return visitors, and sales. You calculate the conversion rate by dividing the number of goals that have been achieved by the number of visits to your website.

**Conversion Rate:** The Conversion Rate is an important aspect of you obtaining your goal of a successful and profitable website. The Conversion Rate is the amount of site visitors that become customers.

**Cost-per-click (CPC):** Cost per click is a term that is used with advertising online. It means the amount of money that the publisher gets every time a visitor to the website clicks on an advertisement. Clicks are counted by their tracking system and then they are paid the agreed upon amount.

**CPM:** CPM is the acronym for cost per thousand; M is the Roman numeral for a thousand. Cost per thousand is used in internet advertisements with banner ads. Banner ads are placed in websites at a agreed upon price per one thousand clicks.

**Group Ads:** The grouping of ads that are connected by a set of keywords.

**Hits:** Hits refers to the amount of times that a webpage is viewed. Large numbers of hits to a website are sometimes misinterpreted as the website being successful but that is not a good metric to measure success. This is because a webpage is made up of many individual files and every request to view an individual file is counted as a hit for the website.

**Impression:** An impression means an advertisement being on a webpage that is being visited. If a webpage has five advertisements, it means five impressions. Impressions are used by web advertisers to see how many views that their advertisements get. Impressions are usually sold by publishers at a cost per thousand (CPM).

**Impressions Rate:** Impressions rate lets you know how many times that your ad was shown in a results search page, which means that it tells you how frequent and competitive a certain search keyword is wanted and how important it is.

**Keyword Bid:** Placing a keyword bid is the act of allotting money to advertising that is associated to a particular keyword. When certain conditions are matched, bids are reviewed with the highest ones selected and then the advertising is shown depending on the bid amounts, the highest first and so on.

**Keyword Density:** Keyword density refers to the amount of times that a keyword or a phase is in an article or a webpage and is usually expressed in percentage. Keyword density can be a key factor with search engine optimization determining if the search keyword will bring up the webpage on the results page. The recommended density for keywords on a webpage or article is fro one to three percent.

**Keyword Stuffing:** Keyword stuffing is to be regarded with suspicion. Keyword stuffing is used by trying to hide text, usually in the same color as the background of a webpage where it is only visible to search engines. However, search engines have developed software that can detect keyword stuffing and will pass over websites that practice it leading to the websites not having any ranking at all.

**Keyword:** A keyword is a term that is used by people searching for something online. They are also important to know if you plan on doing a pay per click campaign. While small companies might have a small amount of keywords that lead people to their site, larger companies will have thousand or more keywords that will lead you to their site.

**Link Building Campaign:** A link building

campaign is when you contact other businesses that are like yours and exchange links with each other on your websites in order to boost both of your rankings on search engines and pay per click campaigns.

**Link Farming:** Link farming is when business exchange links in order to move up the rankings on search engines. However, many search engines to include Google feel that link farming is no better than spam and have come up with ways to detect it and they will not recognize sites that participate in link farming.

**Minimum Bid:** A minimum bid refers to the least amount of money you are willing to pay pre click so that your keyword will show advertisements.

**Opt in e-mail permission marketing:** Opt in e-mail permission marketing is when companies advertise through e-mail only if the recipient of the e-mail has consented to receive such mailings. This gives the company a good database of people who they know have some interest in their products or services.

**Page Rank (PR):** Page rank refers to an amount that gives an estimate of how important a certain webpage is. There are many factors that go into determining the page rank, so it is not necessarily a good indicator of how a page ranks for certain keywords.

**Page Views:** Page views refers to amount of times that a web page has been viewed by a visitor. They are important with online advertising with advertisers using them to know where and when to advertise.

**Paid Inclusion:** Paid inclusion refers to a marketing model with internet search engines. Web sites pay search engines to ensure that their website will be shown when people search for certain keywords. However, most search engine companies have decided to stop this practice.

**Pay Per Click (PPC) Advertising:** Pay per click advertising refers to a type of marketing in which a company pays an agreed upon amount of money every time a person clicks on an advertisement on a search engine results page and is taken to that website.

**Pay Per Click Search Engine (PPCSE):** A pay per click search engine is one that where results are ranked according to bid amounts and advertisers are charged a fee when someone clicks on the search listing.

**Pay Per Performance:** Pay per

performance is an advertising model where the company that is advertising pays a fee to the search engine company dependent on what visitors to their do. If there is no activity then no fee is paid.

**Reciprocal Linking:** Reciprocal linking is when websites link to each other because they sell the same products or services. By having links to other sites, it helps all companies involved to receive a higher page ranking on search engines.

**Return on Investment (ROI):** Return on investment refers to the sum of money that you make when compared to the money that you have spent on a certain topic. Ways to help you calculate how well your return of investment is include using pay per click campaigns.

**Search Engine Friendly:** Search engine friendly refers to websites that have been created with the idea that they are easily accessible to search engines giving them a better chance for a higher ranking on search engine result pages.

**Search Engine Optimization (SEO):** Search engine optimization refers to the methods that are used by using keywords, meta tags, and the changing of content so that websites will receive a higher ranking on search engine results pages.

**Spam:** Spam is basically junk e-mail. It is usually e-mail that has been sent to your e-mail account unsolicited. Most e-mail sites have filters that will stop this type of mail being delivered to your inbox and will go directly to a spam folder or to the trash.

**Unique Visitor:** Unique Visitor refers to a person who visits a website more than one time during a certain period of time. Unique visitors are identified by their IP address and are only counted one time, it does not matter how many time that they visit.

**Vertical Search Engine:** A vertical search engine is a search engine that indexes content by location and topic for consumers or by industry for business to business. Unlike search engines like Yahoo and Google, vertical search engines bring results that are useful to the person doing the search.

**Web Presence:** Web Presence means that a person or a company has established their presence on the Internet, either through e-mail, advertising, blogging, or a website. This term is interchangeable with Internet presence.